A dream has ambition

A powerful force to move you into position

A pathway to excellence and promotion

Though times are challenging

Never sellout but always dedicating

Giving time, energy, and faithfully seeding

Seeding toward a harvest

Manifold blessings of God's best

By faith, speak increase, and see it manifest

It is a beautiful thing to dream

Dream above and beyond with the ability to be redeemed

Never doubt neither fall, but always believe and you will succeed

The structure of a character has mobility

Morals, soundness, and beliefs that brings stability

Gifts of knowledge, wisdom, and understanding that brings you & God in unity

You must learn momentum in life

With humility in heart along with sacrifice

Always using strategy on the enemy, which is your weapon device

Fight the good fight of faith

Balance yourself, be productive, and never faint

Hold on to your good name without a debate

Remember God is never the author of confusion

So do not allow Satan to bring delusions

Keep the fear of God in your heart, keep his commandments, which is the conclusion

CREATION

Creation is the life to all that live
Something we must take to heart
The power of all things made outside and within

Creation is an intervention
Big, small, short or tall
Things you can see through your imagination

The world is surrounded with beauty
When you see it, great joy you'll receive
Respect God's creation and obey which is man's duty

Vapors of water transforms into mist

Not easily seen until transformation is accomplished

Once water appears, life itself becomes sufficient

The need to shed tears and the need of falling rain

Tears for victory, rain for prosperity

Then joy and peace is proclaimed

Staying connected with the Creator

Out of your belly flow rivers of living water from him, the life giver

Water to strengthen not to weaken

Light given and never hidden

A light that shines, not dimmed which God has forbidden

He said let your light so shine

To receive a reward in due time

Receiving this award is not for your glory, God said it is mine

Where there is a voice

There is strength

Strength to stand still or go forward, it's your choice

Express what is in your inner man

There could be something God wants to say

It can be instructions which he always demand

He never wants your opinion

So please don't try to give it

He has the last word and total dominion

A rainbow appears opposite of the sun
As sunlight shines from heaven above
You see life has begun

A rainbow has colors
Green, Red, Blue, Yellow and Purple

A rainbow can form in the rain or mist
As a result we see its creation accomplished

As long as you see a rainbow
You know God's love is alive
This love we know never dies

RAINBOW

A rainbow is a covenant

A promise heaven sent

A promise to secure all his people

Security of life, joy, and love

Life to bring forth good fruit

Life to smell the morning dew

Joy that passes all understanding

And love with perfect meaning

As the raindrops fall

And growth comes

His people must praise him which he has called

So when you see a RAINBOW

Shout "GLORY"

And remember to always abide in God's shadow

THE STRENGTH OF MY MOTHER

THE STRENGTH OF MY MOTHER IS SOMETHING I NEVER THOUGHT I'D GAIN

THROUGH ROUGH & BITTER TIMES
I SAW HER PULL THROUGH AND I TOO LEARNED HOW TO SUSTAIN

SHE MAY NOT KNOW BUT SHE HAS TAUGHT ME HOW TO TRIUMPH & CONQUER
THINGS THAT MAY GET ME DOWN
BUT WHEN I STUDY HER CHARACTER OF STRENGTH THINGS IN LIFE TURNS AROUND

HER HEART SPEAKS WITH WORDS THAT CAN'T EXPRESS
THROUGH THIS I LOOK & SEE HER INNER EMOTIONS THAT SHE CAN NOT CONFESS

ONLY GOD KNOWS HER COMING & HER GOING
BUT I CAN TRULY SAY SUNSHINE ALWAYS CAME THROUGH HER MOURNING

REMEMBERING ALL TRIALS & TRIBULATIONS THAT MADE ME SAD
NOW THAT I'M OLDER I REALIZE EVERYTHING WASN'T SO BAD

MANY THINGS I'VE COMPLAINED ABOUT IN THE PAST THAT CAUSED ME TO SCREAM
BUT THIS IS NOW THE DAY THAT I HAVE REDEEMED

THEREFORE I DONOT HAVE TO SUFFER
AND OWE IT ALL TO THE STRENGTH OF MY MOTHER

A SOUND TO THE EAR IS SENSATIONAL

EASY TO HEAR, EASY TO FEEL

RESTING IN THE ARMS OF A MAN, WHICH IS IRRESISTIBLE

THIS SOUND IS COMPLETE

NOTHING CAN INTERFERE

ANY OTHER YOU CAN DELETE

DEEP PASSION IS A RESULT

SOMETHING YOU CAN CHERISH

RATHER BE ASHAMED WITH FAULT

WHEN YOU HEAR THE SOUND SO GENTLE

KNOW THAT EVERYTHING IS WELL

FOR THIS IS GOD'S SIGNAL

WHEN GOD SPEAKS HE'S MEANT TO BE HEARD

A QUIET STEAL VOICE YOU WILL HEAR

QUICK OBEDIENCE IS WHAT HE PREFERS

NEVER IGNORE HIM, ALWAYS LISTEN

IF YOU FELL TO DO SO

YOU WILL ALWAYS FEEL LIKE SOMETHING IS MISSING

WHOSEVER TAKES HEED HE WILL EXALT

TAKING YOU TO PARADISE

WHERE YOU WOULD NEVER WHAT TO DEPART

SO BE CAREFUL WHAT VOICE YOU PERCEIVE

IT COULD BE A FRIEND OR AN ENEMY

JUST PRAY AND MAKE SURE YOU ARE NOT DECEIVED

POWER

Power is the strength that lies within

To perform the works yet to begin

Power is the leading role to ability

The act of conduct, character and behavior

Anything you desire with capability

Power is a force of energy

You have to pursue

Make haste and create strategy

Using all your might

Lay aside every weight

And put the enemy to a flight

A PASTOR AFTER GOD'S OWN HEART IS A HEART FULL OF GOLD

GOLD FOUND IN A TREASURE THAT YOU AN D I CAN BEHOLD

SHE KNOWS WHAT IS GOOD

SHE KNOWS WHAT IS EVIL

THIS PASTOR DELIVERS GOD'S WORD AS SHE SHOULD

TO GOD SHE TRIES TO BE OBEDIENT

NEVER FALLS OUT OF CHARACTER

ALWAYS WORKING IN MIND AND SPIRIT TO BRING FORTH THINGS THAT ARE MANIFICANT

SHE'S FULL OF WISDOM, KNOWLEDGE, AND UNDERSTANDING

NEVER IS SELFISH BUT IS ALWAYS FORBEARING

A MIND OF SELF CONTROL

A MIND OF STRENGTH

FOCUSED ON GOD'S WILL TO WIN SOULS

WHEN YOU THINK OF A PASTOR AFTER GOD'S OWN HEART

YOU THINK OF HER BECAUSE SHE NEVER GIVES UP BUT ALWAYS PRESSING FORWARD THE MARK

SOUND DOCTRINE IS WHAT SHE TEACHES

TO HELP YOU AND I OVERCOME OUR WEAKNESSES

SHE REACHES OUT TO LOVE AND TO SUPPORT

AS GOD GIVES HER WORDS OF ENCOURAGEMENT

FOR HIS PEOPLE TO COMFORT

TO WANT TRUTH

TO WANT MOTIVATION

SEARCH FOR A PASTOR AFTER GOD'S OWN HEART

"HIDDEN TEARS"

YOUR HIDDEN TEARS ARE SO MANY

HIDDEN FROM FAMILY, FRIENDS BUT IS SEEN ONLY IN THE EYES OF GOD'S SYMPATHY

TEARS YOU MAY THINK SHOW WEAKNESSES

TEARS THAT MAY BRING PAIN & SORROW

BUT AT THE END CREATES MEEKNESS

YOU SOMETIMES FEEL SHEDDING TEARS ARE A WASTE OF TIME

BUT BE NOT DECEIVED, YOUR TEARS COUNT

LEADING TO MIRACLES, WONDERS, & SIGNS

THESE THINGS YOU CANNOT SEE

ONLY GOD KNOWS THE OUTCOME

JUST KEEP WALKING, TRUST GOD & BELIEVE

DON'T BE ASHAME TO SHOW WHO YOU REALLY ARE

SOMEONE MAY NEED TO KNOW

GOD WANTS TO HEAL TROUBLED WOMBS, AS YOU CAN WITNESS BECAUSE HE BROUGHT YOU THIS FAR

NO MORE HIDING BEHIND YOUR TEARS

NO MORE KEEPING SILENT

LET GOD'S LIGHT SHINE ON THEM TO ERASE ALL FEARS

DRIP, DROP LET THEM FLOW

LIKE A STREAM OF LIVING WATER

KNOWING IT LEADS TO YOUR OPEN DOOR

NOW IT'S TIME TO ENTER IN

IT HAS BEEN A LONG JOUNEY, BUT YOU MADE IT SO LET GO OF THOSE THINGS YOU NO LONGER HAVE TO DEFEND

BORN TO BE A MAN

WHEN I LOOK AT YOU I SEE A BIG STATUE

A STATUE THAT SPEAKS OF THINGS OF THE PAST AND PRESENT

HEARING WORDS OF CREATIVITY, SELF- CONFIDENCE, AND POSITIVE ATTITUDE

I WATCHED YOU GROW, I WATCHED YOU LEARN, AND REMEMBERING WHEN I TOLD YOU YES YOU CAN

SEEING THE GIANT IN YOU ALWAYS MADE ME SMILE

KNOWING THE STRENGTH OF YOUR CHARACTER THAT SAYS YOU WERE BORN TO BE A MAN

WHEN YOU KNEW NOT I TAUGHT YOU TO SEEK

WHEN YOU FEARED I TAUGHT YOU FAITH

THEN YOU FOUND OUT WHO YOU REALLY WERE AND REALIZED THE WORDS MOMMA SPEAK

MANY TEARS WE SHED TOGHTER, BUT TURNED OUR MOURNING TO A DANCE

LETTING GO OF ALL THE PAIN AND DISAPPOINTMENTS

MADE US BOTH KNOW YOU WERE BORN TO BE A MAN

CAN YOU STAND STANDING ALONE

STANDING ALONE IS SOMETIMES DIFFICULT

NO ONE IN FRONT NO ONE IN BACK

ALMOST SEEMS YOU'RE IN LACK

YOU MIGHT FEEL AND LOOK AT THINGS THAT MAKE YOU WONDER

THINGS THAT MEAN YOU NO GOOD

THINK IT, FORGET IT AS GOD PUT THOSE THINGS TO ASSUNDER

GO IN THE RIGHT DIRECTION

DISTRACTION IS CONTAGIOUS

AND STAY IN MOTION

KEEP MOVING IN THE WAY OF THE LORD

DON'T QUIT, DON'T TARRY

BE STRONG, COURAGIOUS AND REMAIN MARRY

YES, KEEP YOUR JOY

DON'T LET SATAN PLAY WITH YOUR MIND LIKE A TOY

ALWAYS KNOW HE COMES TO DECEIVE

AND IF YOU FALL PREY

YOU'LL SEE THAT'S JUST WHAT HE CAME TO DO IS TO MISLEAD

HE IS THE AUTHOR OF CONFUSION

WHISPERING LIES IN YOUR EAR

SENDING MAKE BELIEVE FRIENDS TO YOU

BUT REMEMBER THERE'S NO CONNECTION JUST DELUSIONS

NOW THIS YOU MUST KNOW QUITE MAJOR

SO OPEN YOUR EYES TO WHAT'S REAL AND BEHOLD GOD'S FAVOR

THOUGH YOU WITNESS FALSE HOOD AROUND YOU, DON'T HATE

KEEP IN MIND THERE'S NO ONE THAT CAN RELATE

NO ONE BUT GOD CAN BRING YOU CHEER

SO TAKE A STAND AND DON'T FEAR

FAVOR ONLY COMES TO THOSE WHO FEAR GOD AND FOLLOW AFTER HIS WAYS

GETTING AHEAD

SOMEONE MAY ASK YOU; DO YOU WANT TO GET AHEAD?

YOU SAY YES, BUT HOW WITHOUT BEING MISLEAD

YOU WONDER HOW PEOPLE GET A HEAD START

GAINING LOVE AND RESPECT THAT DOESN'T DEPART

SOMETHINGS COME AND SOMETHINGS GO

ONE THING YOU MUST UNDERSTAND

GODS LOVE OUT WEIGHTS THINGS THAT SHOW

YOU WANT TO SEE

YOU WANT TO KNOW

YOU WANT PROOF

BUT ALL YOU NEED IS THE TRUTH

TRUTH COMES

TRUTH NEVER GOES

YOU CAN HOLD ON TO IT

FOR AS THE DAYS ARE LONG

GETTING AHEAD IS GOOD

STARTING OVER ISN'T BAD

JUST KEEP GOD FIRST

AND BE THAT ENGINE THAT COULD

IDENTIFY THE HURT

WHEN YOU HURT THERE IS PAIN

SORROW COMES BUT YOU MUST KNOW WHEN IN DOUBT YOU WILL GAIN

YOU ASK WHAT IS IT TO GAIN WHEN TROUBLES ALL AROUND YOU

YOU CAN'T SEE AHEAD AND YOU DON'T KNOW WHAT TO DO

FIRST IDENTIFY THE HURT AND YOU WILL HEAL

SOMETIMES IT'S EASY SAID THAN DONE

BUT ALWAYS REMEMBER IF YOU DON'T GIVE UP ON YOURSELF VICTORY WILL BE WON

YOUR HEALING IS BASED ON THE WORK YOU PUT IN

JUST IDENTIFY THE IT AND THE HURT WILL HEAL WITHIN

LOVE

LOVE IS JUST LOVE

LOVE CAN SWIM CURRENTLY LIKE A DOVE

LOVE ITSELF CAN SOMETIMES FIT LIKE A GLOVE

LOVE IS LIKE AN UNSOLVED MYSTERY

LOVE IS A DREAM OF REALITY

LOVE IS SOMETHING THAT WHOLES GREAT RESPONSIBLITIES

LOVE IS HELD WITHIN YOUR HEART

LOVE CAN STAND STILL OR DEPART

LOVE IS AN HONOR SO PLEASE BE SMART

LOVE IS NOT A SPORT

LOVE IS MARRIGAE AND NOT DIVORCE

LOVE CAN BE HARD TO DEAL WITH, WHICH LEADS TO REMORSE

LOVE IS ONLY WHAT YOU MAKE IT

LOVE IS TO GIVE AND GET

LOVE IS A FIRE SO KEEP YOURS LIT

PROMISE

PROMISE IS TO FORKEEP

TO ASSURE, TO TRUST

NOT DECEIVE

A WORD SPOKEN

IS A WORD GRANTED

SOMETHING TO EXPECT AS A TOKEN

PROMISE IS A VOW

RECEIVING HOPE, DESIRE, AND WANT

AS WORDS OF HONOR

PROMISE IS HIDDEN TRUTH

DEEP WITHIN YOUR'II FIND

A GROWTH OF THE LIVING WITH DEEP ROOT

PROMISE GUARANTEE'S

SIGN, SEALED, AND WARRANTED

THERE IS A EARNEST NEED TO RECEIVE A PROMISE

FOR CORUAGE, FOR STRENGTH, FOR KNOWLEDGE

LOOKING FOR WHA'T'S TO COME

DARKNESS FOR LIGHT

DEATH FOR LIFE

AN ACT OF SOMETHING SHOWN

THIS PROOF OF A COVENANT

SWORN, GIVEN, NOT TAKEN

THERE'S NO VIOLATION TO A PROMISE

THERE'S NO EMPTINESS TO ITS CAPACITY

BUT FULLNESS OF SUCCESS

IT NEVER TEARS DOWN

IT'S LIFTS UP

LEAVING ROOM TO EXCEL

IF YOU MAKE A PROMISE

YOU KEEP A PROMISE

IT CAN LEAD TO PARADISE

PROMISE HOLDS YOUR FUTURE IN IT' HANDS

SO THE PROMISE YOU MAKE, MAKE IT STAND

SHE'S JUST A LADY

LOOK AT HER WALK

LOOK AT HER HIPS MOVE SIDE TO SIDE

WITH BREAST SO FIRM THAT STANDS LIKE A LIVELY STALK

HER HAIR DARK AND LOVELY

LONG DOWN HER BACK

WITH A SHINE THAT BRINGS ATTRACTIONS MOST DEFINITELY

YOU WONDER WHERE SHE IS GOING

WHAT'S HER MOTIVE

BELIEVE IT OR NOT SHE HAS A PLAN THAT'S NOT ALWAYINGS SHOWING

SHE SITS ON TOP OF THE WORLD

HER CONFIDENCE ENABLES HER TO ACHIEVE HER GOALS

PURSUING HER HEARTS DESIRES THAT NEVER BRINGS BETRAYAL

SHE'S FOCUSED ON WHAT LIFE CAN TEACH HER

LOVE, HAPPINESS, PEACE

THERE'S NO LIMIT THAT'S FOR SURE

SHE LIFT'S UP HER FELOW SISTERS

SPEAKING GOOD WORDS OF LIGHT

THINKING OF HERSELF AS A SUPPORTER

THIS LADY IS NOT JEALOUS

BUT A MOTIVATIONALIST

SHE KNOWS HER WORTH

NOT COMPROMING

NOT SETTLING FOR LESS

BUT GETTING WHAT SHE DESERVES

SHE PROMOTES UNITY

FOOLINESS IS NOT HER NAME

ONLY A WATER FALL OF PEACE

THAT LADY IS SMART

SHE KNOWS ALL THE RIGHT MOVES

HOW TO LIVE, LOVE, WITH NO CHANGE OF HEART

IN PURSUIT OF HAPPINESS

SHE NEVER GIVES UP

SEACHING FOR THE STARS WHICH MAKES HER VICTORIOUS

A SOUND MIND IS WHAT SHE WANTS

NO DISTURBANCES

NO INTERRUPTIONS

ANY SUCH THINGS SHE CONFRONTS

HER HANDS BRING HER WEALTH

SHE KNOWS HOW TO BE CREATIVE

NEVER FORGETTING HER RICHES LYES IN SELF

SHE MEDITATES, SHE DREAMS

PRESSING FORWARD WITH HIGH SELF-ESTEEM

THIS IS THE LADY WE ALL WANT TO KNOW

SO RESPECT HER

LOVE HER

ADORE HER

FOR SHE'S JUST A LADY

SOMETHING TO SMILE ABOUT

THINGS IN THIS WORLD MAY HAPPEN UNEXPECTEDLY

THINGS THAT MAY BRING HURT, BITTNESS AND PAIN

BUT ALWAYS REMEMBER THE GIFT OF LIFE AND THE HAPPINESS THAT IT MAINTAINS

GOD HAS GIVEN US SO MANY THINS TO SMILE ABOUT

MANY TIMES WE TAKE FOR GRANTED HIS TRUE LOVE

LOOKING BACK WE REALIZE THE VICTORY WE WON AND THAT ALONE MAKES YOU SHOUT

SHOUTING IS GOOD WHEN YOU KNOW HOW GOD HAS BROUGHT YOU OUT

MOUNTAINS YOU CLIMBED, HURTLES LEAPED, RACES YOU'VE WON, RIVERS YOU'VE CROSSED

DOES IT ALL ADD UP? YES

YOU HAVE SOMETHING TO SMILE ABOUT

IN LIFE THERE ARE MANY LESSONS TO BE LEARNED

AND THE DECISIONS WE MAKE DOESN'T AIWAYS BRING JOY

WE PAY FOR OUR ACTIONS, THE CONSEQUENCES IS GOD'S WORD CONFIRMED

THIS KEEPS US IN THE ARMS OF GOD

STAYING SAFE FROM ALL HARM AND DANGER

AS BABY JESUS LAID IN A MANAGER

THIS IS WHAT KEEPS ME GOING

NOT GIVING UP, NOT TURNING BACK, NOT LOOKING BEHIND ME

BUT MOVING ALONG JUST AS THE RIVER KEEPS ON FLOWING

THIS IS SOMETHING TO SMILE ABOUT

WHEN YOU NEED A FRIEND

JESUS WILL TAKE YOU IN

KEEPING YOU COMPANY

SO YOU CAN HAVE STABILITY

WHEN YOU SMILE IT BRINGS ON LAUGHTER WHICH BRINGS HEALING AND DELIVERANCE TO YOUR SOUL

TO KNOW THIS

YOU WILL ALWAYS HAVE SOMETHING TO SMILE ABOUT

SUBSTANCE ABUSERS

WE THE BODY OF CHRIST ARE THE TEMPLE OF GOD ELOHIM

WHO REFUSES ALL UNRIGHTEOUS SUPPORT

BUT SOMETIMES COMPROMISES TO AVOID CRITISM

FOR SUPPORT WE SEARCH FOR A VARIETY OF SUBSTANCES

THINGS THAT TEND TO SPOIL US

DELAYING OUR PROMISES AND CREATING ABOMINATIONS

SUDSTANCES DOESN'T CURE TRIBULATIONS, TRAILS, NEITHER SITUATIONS

THE WORD OF GOD IS WHAT MAKES THINGS ALL WELL

ONCE YOU TASTE OF IT YOU WILL NEVER GO HUNGRY, NOT UNDER NO CIRCUMSTANCES

WE LOOK TO THE LEFT AND THE RIGHT

WE RUN FROM OURSELVES AND NEVER LEARN HOW TO FIGHT

WHEN THINGS GO WRONG WE TWIST AND WE TURN

THEN REACHES FOR A SUBSTANCE THAT KILLS OUR SPIRIT

THEN WE FALL AND CAN'T STAND FIRM

WE TAKE THE ADVICE OF UNBELIEVERS

THEN REGRET OUR DECISIONS BECAUSE WE FELL TO BE SEERS

BURDENS BECOME OUR FRIEND

CAN'T GET THE MONKEY OFF YOUR BACK

AND FORGET THE REWARD IS FOR HE THAT ENDURES TO THE END

YOU OUGHT TO COUNT YOUR BLESSINGS AS THEY PRDUCE

NAME THEM ONE BY ONE

AND PUT A END TO SUBSTANCE ABUSE

THIS LOVE I HAVE FOR YOU

THIS LOVE I HAVE FOR YOU IS FROM MY HEART

THIS LOVE I HAVE FOR YOU IS THORN LIKE A DART

THIS LOVE I HAVE FOR YOU WILL NEVER DEPART

THIS LOVE I HAVE FOR YOU ISN'T FALSE

THIS LOVE I HAVE FOR YOU IS BASED ON TRUE CAUSE

THIS LOVE I HAVE FOR YOU IS NOT PLAYED WITH LIKE DOLLS

THIS LOVE I HAVE FOR YOU IS QUITE DIFFERENT

THIS LOVE I HAVE FOR YOU WOULD BE DIFFICULT FOR A INFANT

THIS LOVE I HAVE FOR COMES FROM THE HEART OF INNOCENCE

THIS LOVE I HAVE FOR YOU BRINGS TEARS

THIS LOVE I HAVE FOR YOU BRINGS FEARS

THIS LOVE I HAVE FOR YOU IS ONLY FOR YOUR EARS

THIS LOVE I HAVE FOR YOU IS DELICATED LIKE A FEATHER

THIS LOVE I HAVE FOR YOU WOULD KEEP US TOGETHER

THIS LOVE I HAVE FOR YOU LASTS ALWAYS AND FOREVER

TO CONQUER

TO CONQUER IS TO WIN

POWER TO MOVE BEYOND ALL ODDS

MAINTAINING YOUR HOPE, MAINTAINING YOUR DREAMS YOU NO LONGER DEFEND

LOOKING ON THE BATTLE FIELD

ALL YOUR WEAPONS NEEDED COULDN'T DESTROY YOUR ENEMINES

BUT ONLY YOUR INTERGRITY WAS YOUR SHIELD

SOME DAYS IT TOOK THE LIFE OUT OF YOU TO FIGHT

PAIN, DISTRESS, AND ANIXETY FILLED YOUR HEART

THERE SEEMED TO BE NOTHING TO HOLD ON TO

SO DARK AHEAD NOTHING IN SIGHT

SHAME AND FEAR ALMOST TOOK OVER YOUR SOUL

DOUBT AND GRIEF OF LOSING THE BATTLE WAS NEAR

YET YOUR FLESH WEAK BUT YOUR SPIRIT TOOK CONTROL

AS YOU LOOK AND SAW THE FINISHLINE

YOU KNEW THERE WAS MUCH TO ACCOMPLISH

THEN YOU SAID I MUST PURSUE NO MORE WASTING TIME

BLINDED BY ALL CHAOS YOU DIDN'T SEE YOUR SKILLS

DIGGING DEEP WITHIN YOURSELF

YOU SAW IT ONLY TOOK A SELFWILL

A WILL TO PRESS

A WILL TO BECOME WHOLE

LETTING GO OF ALL STRESS

CLOSE TO THE OPEN DOOR OF STRENGTH AND VIRTUE

NEVER LOOING BACK

RUNNING FAST AS YOU CAN FOR DEPARTURE

LEAVING ALL CARES BEHING

BY ALL MEANS READY TO SHINE

READY TO CONQUER

READY DEFEAT

READY TO MASTER

NOW YOU'RE IN THE SEASON OF CHANGE

AND LIKE YOU ALWAYS WANTED THE SPIRIT OF GAIN

SO BE STEDFAST

STAY THERE AND REMAIN

GOD SPEAKS

GOD YOU SPEAK THROUGH YOUR WORD

THAT WHEN WEAPONS FORMED AGAINST ME I CAN BE PERSREVED

YES I READ YOUR WORD, IT'S IN MY HEART

BUT SOMETIMES WHEN THE BATTLE COMES I'M NOT ALWAYS SMART

GOD YOU REPEAT YOUR WORD TO ME, TO LIVE AND BE A CONQUER

AGAIN I LOSE AND HAVE TO START ALL OVER

I KNOW YOUR MERCY IS EVERLASTING & GREAT

SO IS YOUR GRACE

I JUST DON'T WANT TO CONTINUE TO GRIEVE YOU TO YOUR FACE

LORD CONTINUE TO SPEAK YOUR WORD TO ME

PICK ME UP WHEN I FALL

SO I CAN BE WHO YOU WANT ME TO BE

JUST ASK GOD

THERE ARE MANY QUESTIONS TO ASK

QUESTIONS YOU WANT SO BADLY ANSWERED

HOPING THE OUTCOME WILL LAST

YOU DESIRE SO MUCH IN YOUR HEART

THINGS YOU NEVER HAD, THINGS YOU NEVER SAW

JUST WAITING ON A RESPONSE TO START

AGAINST ALL ODDS

SEEM'S LIKE NO ONE HEARS YOU

JUST ASK GOD

IT'S JUST THAT SIMPLE

HE WILL NOT LET YOU DOWN

WHY? BECAUSE YOU'RE HIS TEMPLE

THE TEMPLE OF THE MOST HIGH

ALL THAT YOU ASK, HE WILL GIVE

HE'S JUST WAITING FOR YOU TO CLIMB

LOOKING AT YOU CLIMB TO THE TOP

WITH OPEN ARMS HE AWAITS

REMEMBER JUST DON'T STOP

BE A WINNER, WIN THIS RACE

BE MOTIVATED, BE READY

TO SEE HIM FACE TO FACE

NEVER DOUBT WHAT YOU ASK THERE IS A REWARD

NOTHING HE WILL WITH HOLD FROM YOU

HE JUST WANT YOU RESTORED

WITH ANSWERED QUESTIONS THERE'S NO NEED TO CRY

JUST WAIT YOUR NIGHT WILL TURN TO DAY

AND THERE WILL BE SUNSHINE, OH MY

NOW IS THE TIME TO ASK GOD

BE BOLD AND GO TO HIS THRONE OF GRACE

REMEMBER WHAT HE GIVES NOTHING CAN ERASE

NOW THAT YOU MADE IT TO HIS DOMAIN

HOLD ON TO HIS UNCHANGING HAND

TO RECEIVE, TO RENEW AND TO GAIN

RICHNESS OF THE HEART

THERE IS WEALTH ALL AROUND YOU

DOORS FLYING OPEN

GRAB A HOLD TO ONE, WALK IN AND SEE WHAT YOU CAN DO

IT DOESN'T HURT TO EXPLORE

WORKING IS THE KEY

IT'S LIKE PERFORMING A CHORE

BELIEVING AS GOD SAID, POWER I GIVE THEE TO GET WEALTH

FAITH IS ALL YOU NEED

HE COMMANDED YOU TO PROSPER AND BE IN GOOD HEALTH

WHERE YOUR HEART IS YOUR TREASURE LIES

IT'S LIKE FOLLOWING AFTER A POT OF GOLD

DIAMONDS, PEARLS, ALL YOU WANT YOU CAN'T DENY

DENYING IS LOSING

JUMPING IS FALLING

LIKE LIFE OR DEATH IT'S YOUR CHOOSING

THE LIGHT THAT SHINES IN A ROOM

A CAR THAT RACES ON THE ROAD

A FRESH SMELL OF PERFUME

YOU MUST FIND THE RICHES IN YOUR HEART

NO SHAME IN YOUR GAIN

SOMETHING YOU CAN TRUST AND NEVER ALLOW TO DEPART

CHALLENGE

THERE IS A CALL TO STIMULTION

BRING FORTH ALL YOU HAVE WITHIN

THINGS THAT WERE ONCE DEAD, BUT NOW LIVES IN ACTIVATION

READY TO LIVE AND READY TO DECLARE

DECLARE WAR ON ALL NEGATIVITY

REACHING FOR GOALS OF YOUR LIFE'S REALITY

YOU SEE THE GOOD COMING ONLY BECAUSE YOU MADE AN EFFORT

YOU'VE BEEN DENIED LONG ENOUGH

THERE'S NO STRUGGLE NOW ONLY COMFORT

THIS IS THE TIME TO BE IDENTIFIED

KNOWING WHO YOU ARE AND SHOWING OTHERS THE SAME

THERE'S NO QUESTION YOU ARE QUALIFIED

CHALLENGE WAS, CHALLENGE TO COME

DON'T WORRY YOU HAVE THE TOOLS

ALL EYES ON YOU THROUGH THE TEST, BUT MAKE NO SENSE TO SOME

PEOPLE WANT TO KNOW HOW YOU ARRIVED

THEY WILL NEVER KNOW

ALL YOU KNOW IS WHAT GOD HAS FOR YOU IT IS FOR YOU BECAUSE OF YOUR STRIVE

YOU OWE NO MAN AN EXPLANATION

GOD HAS FREED YOU

NOTHING STOPPING YOU NOW JUST FULFILLING YOUR OBLIGATION

TO ALL THINGS THERE'S AN END

A START TO A FINISH

BUT ALWAYS REMEMBER GOD THE FATHER WAS AND STILL IS YOUR FRIEND

HE WILL BE YOUR FORCE OF HOPE

NO NEED TO RESIST, GO FOR IT, HE'S ALREADY BROKE THE YOKE

A PRISONER OF SELF

YOU HELD YOURSELF DOWN LONG ENOUGH

HIDING IN GUILT AND SHAME

CAN'T YOU SEE YOU'RE A DIAMOND IN THE ROUGH

YOUR EYES BEHOLD NOTHING BUT DARKNESS

CAN'T SEE BECAUSE OF THE BLIND FOLD

NO CONFIDENCE, NO SELF WORTH, BUT ALL SELF- CONSCIENCE

YOU WANT TO BE FREE

YOU WANT YOUR SHACKLES LOOSE

BUT CAN YOU REALLY SEE

SEE WHERE YOUR'RE REALLY HEADED

SEE WHY YOU'RE IN TO DEEP

DEEP IN DOUDT, FORGETTING THE BLOOD JESUS SHEAD

HIS BLOOD CAN LEAD YOU HOME

BUT YOU'RE THE ONE THAT HAS TO LET GO

LET GO OF DISSAPPOINTMENT AND SEE THROUGH THE CROSS
THE LOVE JESUS SHOWN

LET GO OF THE PRISONER OF SELF

PICK UP YOUR WEAPON AND FIGHT

DESTROY ALL YOUR INNER DEMONS UNTIL NONE IS LEFT

THOUGH YOU'RE SURROUNDED BY BARS

YOU CAN MAKE IT

JUST AWAKE AND HEAR THE SOUND OF THE ALARM

THE ALARM IS TO LEAD YOU OUT OF SIN

THE SOUND OF AN EXODUS

MOVING OUT TO MOVE IN

THE SIN OF UNBELIEF IS DANGEROUS

THAT WILL KEEP YOU BOUND

BUT NOW YOU ARE NO LONGER A PRISONER OF SELF

WALK OUT AND BEGAN TO USE YOUR GIFT

TO SEE, YOU MUST LOOK

WHEN YOU SEE, YOU MUST LOOK

LOOKING AT THE INVISIABLE AND THE VISIABLE

WANTING TO TAKE CONTROL OF YOUR DREAMS YOU'RE SO LONG FORSOOK

TAKING WHAT HAS ALWAYS BEEN YOURS

BY FORCE KNOCKING DOWN BARRIERS AND WALLS

GAINING OWNERSHIP OF THE NEW AND CLOSING OLD ALL DOORS

SEEING THE CHANGES MANIFEST BEFORE YOUR EYES

ENTERING INTO A PLACE OF EASE AND COMFORT

OH WHAT A SURPRISE

THIS PLACE YOU FIND MORE HOPE AND STRENGTH

TO RECEIVE ALL BLESSINGS

IT'S LIKE GOING UP A LATTER OR FENCE

CLIMBING ALL THE WAY TO THE TOP

WITH JOY IN YOUR HEART

NEVER WANTING TO STOP

SOMEONE THEN ASK YOU, WHERE ARE YOU GOING?

YOU REPLY, I'M GOING WHEREEVER THE SPIIRIT LEADS ME

HOPING TO GAIN ALL TERRITORY THAT I SEE

YES IT'S ALL MINE

BECAUSE I'VE WAITED SO LONG FOR THIS EXPERIENCE

AND NOW IT'S TIME FOR ME TO SHINE

I'VE LOOKED AND NOW I SEE

MY FAITH HAS OVER TAKEN ME

SO NOW WHEN YOU SEE ME COMING

YOU'LL SEE VICTORY AND NOT DEFEAT

TO SEE YOU MUST LOOK

TO FIND YOU MUST SEEK

ALL THE TREASURE BELONGS TO YOU

IT'S JUST SOMETHING YOU MUST DO

AND THAT IS TO SEE, YOU MUST LOOK

LOOKING OUT THE WINDOW

YOU'RE INSIDE LOOKING OUT OF THE WINDOW

AFRAID TO SEE, AFRAID TO KNOW

ALL ALONE JUST YOU AND YOUR SHADOW

NO EXPECTION, NO COURAGE

NO LIGHT ONLY DARKNESS

SOUNDS LIKE A SHORTAGE

NOTHING TO PUSH YOU OUT

NO SIGN OF MOTIVATION

NO RAIN ONLY DIM CLOUDS

RAIN REPRESENTS THE FLOW OF BLESSINGS

BLESSINGS YOU WILL NEVER SEE

BECAUSE OF YOUR LACK OF INTEGRITY

YOU SEEM TRAPPED WITHIN

WITH NO VOICE TO HEAR

PLEASE WAKE UP AND TRY AGAIN

SEARCH FOR AN EXIT

SOMETHING AWAITS YOU

JUST GO AND GET IT

LOOKING OUT THE WINDOW DOESN'T HELP

NO ONE CAN LEAD THE WAY, ONLY YOU

YES JUST YOURSELF

THE OPEN DOOR IS NOT FAR TO REACH

BE BRAVE DON'T FEAR

NO FEELING OF LOSING NEITHER DEFEAT

THIS IS YOUR ONLY CHANCE

TIME AND OPPORTUNITY IS YOURS

LISTEN TO YOUR INNER MAN TELL YOU, YES YOU CAN

YOU CAN CLOSE THE WINDOW

SHUT THE DOOR OF HOPELESSNESS

AND BEGAN TO SEE WHAT YOU'RE MISSED AND BE GRATEFUL

NO MORE LOOKING OUT THE WINDOW

YOU'RE DREAMS YOUR GOALS ARE NOW IN FRONT OF YOU

READY SET GO

DESTINY

THERE IS A PLACE WE ALL LOOK FORWARD TO GOING

TO SETTLE DOWN AND BE WHAT GOD DESIGNED US TO BE

THIS DOESN'T HAPPEN OVERNIGHT

THERE'S A PREDETERMINED COURSE OF EVENTS

THEN WHAT SEEMS SO FAR OFF SEEMS SO BECOMING

THIS JOURNEY LEADS TO A FORTUNE

EVERYONE HAS A CHANCE TO RECEIVE PROSPEROUSLY

AS SURE AS THE SUN SHINES OVER THE EARTH, YES YOU HAVE YOUR PORTION

THE POWER TO KNOW IS FOR CERTAIN

ONE CAN DECREE A THING FOR SURE

ALL REVEALED JUST LIKE A OPEN CURTAIN

MANY OUTCOMES, MANY RESULTS

THIS PLACE YOU CAN'T DETOUR

A SUPPOSED, A PROPHETIC FORCE

DESTINY IS WHAT YOU CALL IT

THE END TO ALL AGONY, PAIN, AND HURT

NO ACCIDENT ALL INTENT

TO REACH THIS EXPECTED GOAL

THERE IS A RACE YOU MUST RUN

BECAUSE DESTINY AWAITS AND YOU MUST GO

THE BLESSINGS OF GOD BEATS LUCK

YOU CAN COUNT ON HIM

KNOWING ALL THINGS HE HANDLES AND NEVER FORSOOK

ONCE YOU MEET DESTINY

THERE IS NO ESCAPE

GOOD OR BAD IT'S FOR KEEPS

www.ingramcontent.com/pod-product-compliance
Ingram Content Group UK Ltd.
Pitfield, Milton Keynes, MK11 3LW, UK
UKHW061830190726
13855UKWH00005B/1733